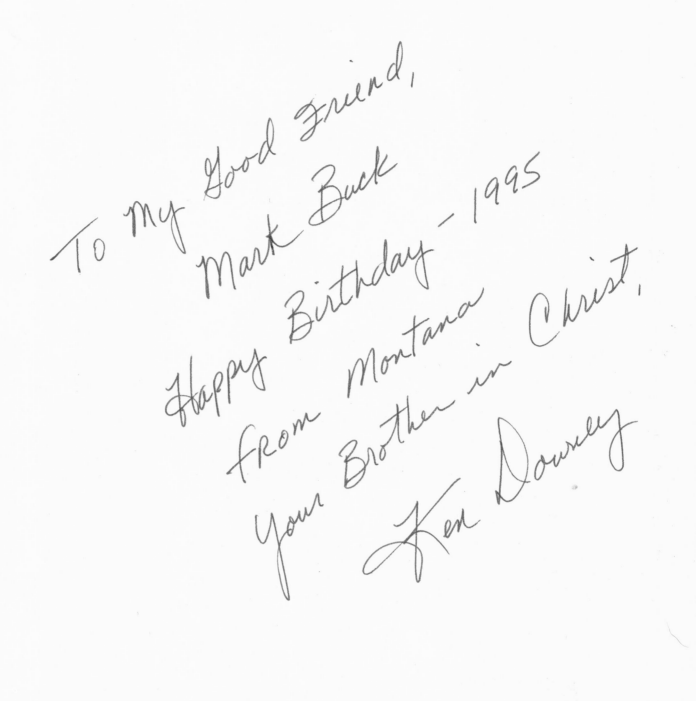

To My Good Friend,

Mark Buck

Happy Birthday - 1995

from Montana

Your Brother in Christ,

Ken Downey

MONTANA
THE LAST BEST PLACE

Photography by Michael S. Sample
and other outstanding photographers

Published by

FALCON PRESS®

In cooperation with

Missoulian   **The Montana Standard**

Autumn colors along the Yellowstone River and 10,960-foot Emigrant Peak in Paradise Valley, south of Livingston   MICHAEL S. SAMPLE

The story of
MONTANA: THE LAST BEST PLACE

From Falcon Press

In 1987, Falcon Press published *Montana on My Mind*, a large-format, full-color tribute to the state in words and photos. Almost overnight, this hardcover book became a best seller.

In 1988, the Montana Historical Society published *The Last Best Place: A Montana Anthology*, a stunning collection of superb writing from the state's finest writers, past and present. This book soon became the best-selling literary anthology on Montana.

Both books celebrated Montana–its tremendous natural beauty, its grand sweep of space and sky, its unique spirit of rugged individualism tempered by neighborliness and a shared sense of community.

Now, in cooperation with the Montana Historical Society, we are proud to present *Montana: The Last Best Place*, a book inspired by *Montana on My Mind* and *The Last Best Place*. Here, we have combined the very best of Montana–the finest writers, the most stunning images. The result is a heartfelt portrait of Montana, the "last best place" that we are fortunate enough to call home.

We hope you enjoy it.

Michael S. Sample and Bill Schneider, Publishers
Falcon Press

From the Montana Historical Society

The Montana Historical Society is pleased to acknowledge Falcon Press's new book, *Montana: The Last Best Place*, as a tribute to *The Last Best Place* literary anthology, orginally published as a celebration of Montana's heritage during the state's cultural centennial year in 1989. It is, indeed, a welcome event when a Montana publisher undertakes to support Montana by producing a superb tribute to the state and its great literary heritage. Just as the Society's anthology, a critical success and surprise best seller, helped make Montana the last best place through words, Falcon Press's new book helps do the same through pictures and excerpts from *The Last Best Place* anthology.

Montana: The Last Best Place is a welcome addition to the ever-growing roster of books about Montana.

Lawrence Sommer, Director
Montana Historical Society

Alpine wildflowers forming a streamside garden near the Garden Wall, Glacier National Park   MICHAEL JAVORKA

The boulder-studded Madison River in the Beartrap Canyon, near Norris   MICHAEL S. SAMPLE

Reaching the far side of the Stillwater River near Absarokee   MICHAEL S. SAMPLE

Wood lily blossoms   ERWIN & PEGGY BAUER

Mule deer fawn exploring a field of ferns   ERWIN & PEGGY BAUER

Butterfly and blanketflower   MICHAEL S. SAMPLE

Sprinkler fun on a hot summer day in Polson   SCOTT SPIKER

Montana weather: sunshine on the National Bison Range, storm clouds over the Mission Mountains   MICHAEL S. SAMPLE

Skier's delight: carving turns in sparkling powder WILLIAM R. SALLAZ

Exploring a snow cave MICHAEL JAVORKA

The Middle Fork of the Flathead River, often called Montana's wildest river   MICHAEL S. SAMPLE

Face-to-face with a mountain goat   MICHAEL S. SAMPLE

Reflections of a red fox   TOM & PAT LEESON

WHY MONTANA IS THE LAST BEST PLACE

By Mike Mansfield

In the hearts and minds of many people–both Montanans and those who live elsewhere– Montana is the last best place. Why? It is the land, the weather, the history, the people–it's all of these elements and more–and it's the way these elements blend together in remarkable ways to create the last best place.

The bond that ties Montanans to the state is woven of many strands. But, before all else, it involves our personal feelings and our pride, as citizens of the state, for its beauty, history, and people.

To us, Montana is a symphony.

It is a symphony of color. It is painted by a thousand different plants and shrubs which set the hills ablaze–each with its own kind of inner fire–during spring and summer. Montana is the intense blue of the Big Sky reflected in the deep blue of mountain lakes and the ice-blue of tumbling streams. It is the solid white of billowing clouds and the haze-white of snow on a hundred mountain peaks. It is the infinite theme of green in mile after mile of farm-rich valleys and in millions of acres of forests.

We who are of Montana know the color harmony of a springtime of millions of wildflowers–the orange poppies, purple heather, yellow columbines, red Indian paintbrush, beargrass, and purple asters in the mountains; the tiger lilies, dogtooth violets, mariposa lilies, bitterroot and kinnikinnick in the foothills; the shooting stars, daisies, larkspur, yellow bells, and sand lilies in the plains.

And in the long winter we know the muted music of the snows which blanket the state. A theme of hope runs through these snows because they are the principal storehouse of the state's great natural resource of water. In one year the amount which will flow out of the mountains and rush down the hills is enough to fill Montana from boundary to boundary to a depth of six inches. And bear in mind that Montana's 54 million acres make the state larger than the entire nation of Japan with its 122 million people compared to our 800,000.

Montana is a symphony. It is a symphony of color and it is a symphony of sounds. Listen for them for a moment, in the names of places. There are mountain ranges called the Beaverhead, the Sapphire, the Ruby, the Bears Paw, the Highwoods, the Snowies, the Beartooths, the Judiths, the Crazies, and the Big Belts. And, incidentally, there are also the Little Belts as well.

There are streams whose names sing: the Silver Bow, the Flathead, the Kootenai, and the Sun; the Jefferson, the Madison, the Gallatin, and the

Dawn of a cowboy's day   WILLIAM R. SALLAZ

Moonset behind Meeteetse Spires, a Nature Conservancy preserve near Red Lodge   MICHAEL S. SAMPLE

Hanging Gardens at Logan Pass, the highest point along the Going-to-the-Sun Road, Glacier National Park MICHAEL JAVORKA

Musselshell; the Milk, the Yellowstone, the Tongue, the Powder, the Blackfoot, and the Boulder.

And when the roll of Montana's cities and towns is called, you hear: Eureka, Chinook, Whitefish, Cut Bank; Circle, Hungry Horse, Absarokee, Butte, Wolf Point, and Great Falls. And you hear Lodge Grass, Lame Deer, Deer Lodge, Crow Agency, Big Fork, and Twodot.

These and a hundred others like them are strains in the history of the state. Each has a story, and together they sing the story of Montana.

It began in a mist of time, with Indians—with the Crows, the Blackfeet, the Assiniboine, the Flatheads, the Chippewa-Crees, the Sioux, and the Northern Cheyennes. Then came Lewis and Clark and the great fur-trading companies. When the boom in pelts died, the gold rush began. At Grasshopper Creek in 1862, the find was so rich it was said the miners could pull up sage brush and shake a dollar's worth of dust out of the roots. The town of Confederate Gulch grew on gold. In six years the population jumped from zero to 10,000 people. In the seventh year, the gold was gone, and only 64 lonely souls remained.

Indians, fur and gold echo in the overture to Montana's history and throughout runs the beat of the famous and infamous, the hunted, the haunted, the violent and the pacific and the politic.

Bald eagle striking a regal pose   TOM & PAT LEESON

Blackfeet dancer at North American Indian Days in Browning
MICHAEL JAVORKA

Family conference: whitetail doe and three fawns   DONALD M. JONES

Canada geese and goslings   MICHAEL S. SAMPLE

Bright-eyed black bear cub   TOM & PAT LEESON

Hiking on the edge of the Absaroka-Beartooth Wilderness   LINDA CAUBLE

Puppy play during a fishing trip on the Gallatin River   DENVER A. BRYAN

Silver came after gold. Then it was copper's turn, at Butte and Anaconda in western Montana. While some dug into Montana's earth for wealth, others sought it from what grew out of the earth. Stockmen filled the rolling, grass-covered high plains of central and eastern Montana with cattle and sheep. In scarcely ten years the cattle population rose from a few thousand to over a million. Then the cruel winter of 1886-87 froze 90 percent of them into grotesque ice sculptures on the plains, and another Montana "boom" went "bust."

Beginning in the 19th century, railroads ran through the symphony of Montana.

Montanans drove, tumbled and stumbled into the 20th century. The state has picked itself up and started over again many times. Its history is of a people drawn from many sources, headed toward the glowing promise of the Western Frontier. It is of a people who have known the collapse of hope and the renewal of hope. It is of a people who have lived in intimacy with fear as well as courage, with cruelty as well as compassion. It is of a people who have known not only the favor but the fury of a bountiful and brooding Nature. The history of Montana is the song of a people who, repeatedly shattered, have held together, persevered, and, at last, taken enduring root.

Now the 20th century moves on toward the 21st, and the ups and downs of the past yield to the more stable present. Plane travel cuts the huge distances and the immense isolation. Indeed, the virtues of Montana's space, clean air, and clean water, scenery and unparalleled recreational opportunities are becoming better known and look ever more inviting to the rest of the nation.

Modern transitions notwithstanding, something remains in the state that is durably unique and uniquely durable. It is to be found in the character of the people. Montanans are formed by the vastness of a state whose mountains rise to 12,000 feet in granite massives, piled one upon another as though by some giant hand. To drive across the state is to journey, in distance, from Washington, D.C., north to Toronto or south to Florida. In area, we can accommodate Virginia, Maryland, Delaware, Pennsylvania and New York, and still have room for the District of Columbia.

Yet, in all this vastness, we are far less than a million people. In short, Montanans have room to live, to breathe, and above all, to think–to think with a breadth of view which goes to the far horizon and beyond. Vast and empty space and high mountains may isolate a population, but they open the minds of a people. The minds of Montanans dwell not only upon community and state, but upon the nation and the world and on the essential unity of all. And this sense of unity is buttressed by the harsh uncertainties of an all-powerful environment which has taught us to draw together in a mutual concern for one another and to be hospitable to all who come from afar.

■ ■ ■

Sunrise on the Yellowstone River near Pompey's Pillar,
a landmark named by Lewis and Clark
MICHAEL S. SAMPLE

Springtime view of the Mission Mountains from the Swan Valley   MICHAEL S. SAMPLE

Ski mountaineering in the Swan Range, Flathead National Forest   MICHAEL JAVORKA

M ontana's special gift is space, landscape made personal; space

that reaches out to the horizon then comes back and gets under your

skin. It reaches inward, wraps itself around your soul, incubates and

grows. When you finally begin to understand just what it is about

Montana that is important to you, it has already taken root in your

heart and you'll never be the same.

Glenn Law, from "More Than Skin Deep" in *Montana Spaces*

Winter-clad crown of the continent: peaks of the Northern Rockies in the Bob Marshall Wilderness and Glacier National Park   MICHAEL S. SAMPLE

The Swan River flowing swift and clear near Condon   MICHAEL S. SAMPLE

A peaceful section of the Blackfoot, the river in Norman Maclean's *A River Runs Through It*   MICHAEL S. SAMPLE

*T*he voices of the subterranean river in the shadows were different

from the voices of the sunlit river ahead. In the shadows against the

cliff the river was deep and engaged in profundities, circling back on

itself now and then to say things over to be sure it had understood

itself. But the river ahead came out into the sunny world like a

chatterbox, doing its best to be friendly. It bowed to one shore

and then to the other so nothing would feel neglected.

Norman Maclean, from *A River Runs Through It* in *The Last Best Place*

A portion of the 71-mile-long Bighorn Canyon National Recreation Area south of Hardin   SALVATORE J. VASPOL

Bird hunters on the prairie north of Lewistown   BUD JOURNEY

For hundreds of miles nothing

turns or breaks the wind. The land

lies stark and flat under a thin sky

that doesn't touch down at the horizon,

just disappears in the distance.

Barbed wire sings songs here.

Glenn Law, from "More Than Skin Deep"
in *Montana Spaces*

Overland by wagon train near Wolf Point   GARRY WUNDERWALD

Western tanager decorating a barbed-wire fence   MICHAEL S. SAMPLE

Rolling plains near the Chief Joseph Battleground of the Bear's Paw in north-central Montana   JOHN REDDY

T he Great Plains which I cross in my sleep are bigger than any

name people give them. They are enormous, bountiful, unfenced,

empty of buildings, full of names and stories. They extend beyond

the frame of the photograph. Their hills are hipped, like a woman

asleep under a sheet. Their rivers rhyme. Their rows of grain

strum past. Their draws hold springwater and wood and game

and grass like sugar in the hollow of a hand.

Ian Frazier, from *Great Plains*

Badlands on the Charles M. Russell National Wildlife Refuge, south of Fort Peck Lake   MICHAEL S. SAMPLE

Prickly pear cactus blossom   MICHAEL S. SAMPLE

Pheasant hunting in a prairie draw   JEFF VANUGA

Birch Lake, one of nearly three dozen lakes in Jewel Basin Hiking Area, Flathead National Forest   MICHAEL S. SAMPLE

*B*ecause Montana is so dissimilar from border to border and from county to county, there must be other

reasons for our shared sense of identity and literature besides lists of favorite places. And the foremost of these

reasons is, I think, an unconscious but still active sense of the frontier.... We know, even if we never go there,

that the great Beartooth Range rises only a few hours to the east, that only a few miles west the rugged

beauty of the Rocky Mountain Front meets the plains still frequented by grizzlies. Rising like sets of magical

backdrops, Montana's mountains bear physical witness that we live in a largely unsettled, harsh, and fragile

land in the foreground of even wilder, less hospitable distances.

Ralph Beer, from "In Spite of Distance" *in Montana Spaces*

Cap rocks in 8,934-acre Makoshika State Park, Montana's largest state park, near Glendive   MICHAEL S. SAMPLE

Sunset over the Absaroka Mountains north of Yellowstone National Park   SALVATORE J. VASPOL

Ramparts of the Rocky Mountain Front, including 9,066-foot Chief Mountain (left) near the
Blackfeet Indian Reservation   MICHAEL S. SAMPLE

End of the day on 27-mile-long Flathead Lake, largest natural freshwater lake in the western United States   TOM & PAT LEESON

Fragrant water lilies on Salmon Lake
MICHAEL S. SAMPLE

33

Hardy junipers surviving on a red hillside in the Pryor Mountains
MICHAEL S. SAMPLE

Spring was coming even if the weather didn't know it. A week of good weather and the cottonwoods would bust their buttons and the diamond willow run out leaves as narrow as snakes' tongues, and at sundown a man would hear the killdeer crying. Spring made a man feel good and sad, too, and wild sometimes, wanting to howl with the wolves or strike north with the ducks or fork a horse and ride alone over the far rim of the world into new country, into a fresh life. Spring was a good hurting inside the body. It made laughter come easy, and tears if a man didn't shut them off.

A. B. Guthrie, Jr., from *The Big Sky*
in *The Last Best Place*

Spring stroll near the Mission Mountains Wilderness
MICHAEL JAVORKA

Cow elk and newborn calf   DENVER A. BRYAN

34

Clear cascades on Reynolds Creek in Glacier National Park   MICHAEL S. SAMPLE

Spring beauties: Indian paintbrush, arnica, and Lewis monkeyflower along the Continental Divide   LARRY ULRICH

Early autumn along the North Fork of the Flathead River   GEORGE SCHUYLER

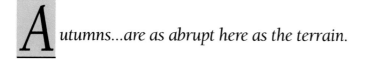 *utumns...are as abrupt here as the terrain.*

David Long, from "Eclipse" in *The Last Best Place*

Brilliant autumn colors below the Garden Wall, Glacier National Park   JOHN REDDY

Fall fishing on a cool day along the Yellowstone River   MICHAEL S. SAMPLE

Bull elk and two cows in the Montana portion of Yellowstone National Park MICHAEL S. SAMPLE

Netting a brown trout in the Gallatin River DENVER A. BRYAN

Hand-hewn homesteader's cabin in southwestern Montana   MICHAEL S. SAMPLE

*A*s *I looked across the rolling expanse of prairie, fired with the beauty of a Montana sunset, I sent up*

a little prayer of thanksgiving from my heart for this, our very first home. Only a rectangle of prairie sod,

raw and untouched by the hand of man, but to us it was a kingdom. I loved the prairie, even while I feared it.

God's country, the old-timers called it. There is something about it which gets a man—or a woman. I feared

its relentlessness, its silence, and its sameness, even as I loved the tawny spread of its sun-drenched ridges,

its shimmering waves of desert air, the terrific sweep of the untrammeled wind.... Still in my dreams I can

feel the force of that wind, and hear its mournful wail around my shack in the lonely hours of the night.

Pearl Price Robertson, from "Homestead Days in Montana" in *The Last Best Place*

Frost crystals refracting morning sunlight on prairie grass MICHAEL S. SAMPLE

Fiery sunset along the road to Hell Creek Recreation Area on Fort Peck Lake, north of Jordan MICHAEL S. SAMPLE

Squatter's rights: a marmot at home in an abandoned homestead
TOM & PAT LEESON

The thirty-foot cliffs of the Madison Buffalo Jump, a *pishkun* used by Native Americans for nearly 2,000 years   MICHAEL S. SAMPLE

W*e did not think of the great open plains, the beautiful rolling hills,*

the winding streams with tangled growth as wild. Only to the white man

was nature a wilderness, and only to him was the land infested with wild

animals and savage people. To us it was tame. The earth was beautiful

and we were surrounded with blessings of the great mystery.

Luther Standing Bear, Oglala Sioux

Fog-shrouded bison in Yellowstone National Park   MICHAEL S. SAMPLE

Custer's tombstone at the Little Bighorn Battlefield
National Monument   MICHAEL CRUMMETT

A Northern Cheyenne in traditional dress   MICHAEL S. SAMPLE

Pronghorn antelope cresting a prairie ridge at sunset   MICHAEL S. SAMPLE

Elk pictograph in central Montana   MICHAEL S. SAMPLE

A long-tailed weasel standing tall   MICHAEL S. SAMPLE

Belt Creek east of Great Falls   MICHAEL S. SAMPLE

Ranch country between Big Timber and Harlowton   TOM & PAT LEESON

*T*he nucleus of family is part of what gives ranching its special identity....

If you're a rancher you're somebody, particularly if the ranch has been

in the family for some generations. But ranchers are not elitists. They work

with their hands. They have manure on their boots. Yet in the eyes

of many they warrant distinction because they have something a lot of people

would like to have, like the chance to ride horses and work cattle, to be their

own boss on their own place, and to be keeper of the legendary West.

Scott Hibbard, from "A Matter of Blood" in *Montana Spaces*

Moving the herd during the Centennial Cattle Drive   MICHAEL S. SAMPLE

One ranching generation leading another   JOHN REDDY

Twin lambs and proud sheepherder near Beaver Creek
MICHAEL CRUMMETT

Not a good place to land at the Dillon Labor Day Rodeo   WILLIAM R. SALLAZ

Modern-day watering hole   WILLIAM R. SALLAZ

Barrel racing with style at the Crow Fair Rodeo, Crow Agency
MICHAEL CRUMMETT

Cowboys finishing a long day's work near Choteau   MICHAEL JAVORKA

Gathering at the cook wagon on the Centennial Cattle Drive   MICHAEL CRUMMETT

Young rider in the Crow Fair Parade at Crow Agency
MICHAEL CRUMMETT

Strutting sage grouse   MICHAEL S. SAMPLE

Snowy peaks of the Crazy Mountains rising above cattle country
north of Big Timber   MICHAEL S. SAMPLE

Wind-shaped snowdrifts along the Rocky Mountain Front near East Glacier   MICHAEL S. SAMPLE

Winter in the Big Hole Valley   MICHAEL S. SAMPLE

Feeding cattle from a horse-drawn hay wagon near Avon   MIKE LOGAN

White on white, near Columbus   MICHAEL S. SAMPLE

*B*ecause the climate is harsh, the geography unforgiving, and the economy often Spartan, it's natural to assume that living in Montana is hard. "You gotta be tough to live in Montana." You hear it time and time again.... But you don't have to be tough to live where the air is clean, water pure, and it will be a cold day in hell before a nuclear reactor moves in next door. It is comfortable living where your spirit and space can reach to the horizon or linger along a trout stream. Living in Montana is easy. Leaving it is hard.

Glenn Law, from "More Than Skin Deep" in *Montana Spaces*

55

Challenging "The Ridge" at Bridger Bowl   BOB ALLEN

Bighorn sheep above Swiftcurrent Lake, Glacier National Park   MICHAEL S. SAMPLE

Ski touring in the northeast corner of Yellowstone National Park,
near Cooke City   MICHAEL S. SAMPLE

Song dog: a coyote in full voice   TOM & PAT LEESON

Spectacular flying dismount at the Miles City Bucking Horse Sale   MICHAEL CRUMMETT

Cowboy bulletin board in Jordan   MICHAEL CRUMMETT

Hiking in the Cabinet Mountains Wilderness near Libby MICHAEL S. SAMPLE

Laying in firewood near Lindbergh Lake in the Swan Valley
MICHAEL S. SAMPLE

Washing off trail dust in a stock tank
MICHAEL CRUMMETT

Autumn anglers at Big Salmon Lake in the Bob Marshall Wilderness   MICHAEL S. SAMPLE

Snow ghost and skier at Big Mountain near Whitefish
DIANE ENSIGN

S pace becomes personal in Montana, a

possession, something held in the heart like a

favorite view or remembered scene. There's

enough space in the state, and few enough people;

everyone might well have a favorite view all to

themselves and never have to share it with

another. The urgency of space is something that

is shared, yet remains intensely personal....

It becomes a possession and like any possession

that is precious and valuable,

it is carefully guarded.

Glenn Law, from "More Than Skin Deep"
in *Montana Spaces*

Horseback trip along the Chinese Wall in the heart of the
Bob Marshall Wilderness   BILL CUNNINGHAM

View of the Missouri River from an 1805 campsite of
Lewis and Clark, near Three Forks   BUD JOURNEY

Enjoying the float-away freedom of dandelion seeds in Polson   SCOTT SPIKER

Campfire magic: mesmerized by dancing flames   MICHAEL S. SAMPLE

Serpentine ice along the Yellowstone River, Riverfront Park in Billings   MICHAEL S. SAMPLE

Plowed fields holding snow in open country near Dillon   ART WOLFE

As soon as he stepped off the train he knew it was what he'd been looking

for. He had the sense of being set free. Of not being hemmed in. He could see

and breathe. Any nobody was standing at his elbow telling him to do this and

that. "I'd finally got out of the woods," he said. He certainly had. You could

look and look, no trees except a thin line of brush along the creek, all else

prairie and sky. There were mountains on the horizon, but offering no limits,

you knew there was plenty of open country beyond.

Dan Cushman, from "A Toad in Hell" in *The Last Best Place*

Skytop Lakes and Glacier on the Beartooth Plateau north of Cooke City   MICHAEL S. SAMPLE

Montana's state flower, the bitterroot   MICHAEL S. SAMPLE

Bighorn ram fording the Gardner River in Yellowstone
National Park, near Gardiner   MICHAEL S. SAMPLE

A portion of the vast Selway-Bitterroot Wilderness crowned by 9,983-foot El Capitan MICHAEL S. SAMPLE

A rainbow arching over a road north of Laurel   MICHAEL S. SAMPLE

Meeteetse Spires near Red Lodge   MICHAEL S. SAMPLE

Foggy summer morning near Cascade   WILLIAM R. SALLAZ

As the land is a living entity it must be worked with rather than

worked on. It requires a melding of human effort with the land's

natural propensity to grow things. Therein lies the art.

Scott Hibbard, from "A Matter of Blood" in *Montana Spaces*

Shiny and green, winter wheat growing in early spring near Bozeman   MICHAEL S. SAMPLE

Shades of the Old West: the Wild Horse Race at the Livingston Rodeo   PAUL DIX

Sunrise silhouettes between East Glacier and Browning   MICHAEL S. SAMPLE

Sunning session on ranchhouse steps near the Bears Paw
Mountains   MICHAEL CRUMMETT

Barnyard buffet near Boulder   DARRIN A. SCHREDER

Prairie earth and sky between Fort Benton and Highwood   MICHAEL S. SAMPLE

The feel of the country settled into Jim,

the great emptiness and age of it, the feel of

westward mountains old as time and plains

wide as forever and the blue sky flung

across. The country didn't give a damn

about a man or any animal. It let the

buffalo and the antelope feed on it and the

gophers dig and the birds fly and men crawl

around, but what did it care, being one

with time itself?

A. B. Guthrie, Jr., from *The Big Sky* in *The Last Best Place*

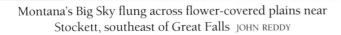

Montana's Big Sky flung across flower-covered plains near
Stockett, southeast of Great Falls JOHN REDDY

Wrangling horses and mules on a pack trip in the northern section of Yellowstone National Park   JEFF HENRY

Bison cows and calf, National Bison Range   MICHAEL S. SAMPLE

Pasqueflowers   MICHAEL S. SAMPLE

Primeval scene: bull moose browsing in Yellowstone National Park   MICHAEL S. SAMPLE

Vivid fall colors in an aspen grove   MICHAEL S. SAMPLE

S ummers' gray eye slipped from Boone to Uncle Zeb. "She ain't sp'iled,

Zeb," he said quietly. "Depends on who's lookin'." "Not sp'iled! Forts all up

and down the river, and folk everywhere.... And greenhorns comin' up, a heap

of 'em—greenhorns on every boat, hornin' in and sp'ilin' the fun.... God, she

was purty onc't. Purty and new.... " It was beginning to get dark. The fire in

the west was about out; low in the east one star burned. Boone heard his own

voice, sounding tight and toneless. "She still looks new to me, new and purty."

A. B. Guthrie, Jr., from *The Big Sky* in *The Last Best Place*

A perfect autumn day in the Absaroka Mountains east of Livingston   MICHAEL S. SAMPLE

Spring snowmelt on the 10,000-foot Beartooth Plateau, the high roof of Montana   MICHAEL S. SAMPLE

Cow moose crossing a high-country pond in the Madison Range   MICHAEL S. SAMPLE

Forest hunter: a lynx in northwestern Montana   ART WOLFE

Floating the Smith River between Camp Baker and Eden Bridge, a 61-mile trip   MICHAEL S. SAMPLE

*D*elightful Montana, a land of distances and of alpine heights, a paradise

of lake and forest, snow-tipped mountains and broad vistas of rolling valley

and plain, invites weary city folk and dwellers of the flat spaces to come and

learn the real meaning of the word "recreation."

Montana, Tourist Edition 1921

Fishing a spring creek in Paradise Valley south of Livingston   ERWIN & PEGGY BAUER

Rainbow trout in the crystal-clear West Fork of the
Stillwater River   MICHAEL S. SAMPLE

Cooling off after hiking to Crescent Lake in the Mission
Mountains   MICHAEL S. SAMPLE

Hunter's dawn over duck decoys near Toston   MIKE LOGAN

Pack train in Kootenai National Forest above the Yaak Valley   DONALD M. JONES

Hikers taking a scenic break atop Headquarters Pass in the "Bob" (Bob Marshall Wilderness)   MICHAEL S. SAMPLE

Floating the White Cliffs section of the Wild and Scenic
Missouri River   MICHAEL S. SAMPLE

Successful anglers   LINDA CAUBLE

83

Sailboarding across Canyon Ferry Lake   WILLIAM R. SALLAZ

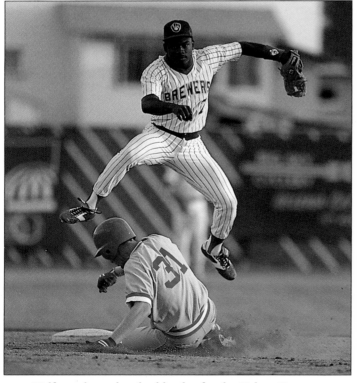

Halfway through a double play for the Helena Brewers
WILLIAM R. SALLAZ

Skaters at the United States High Altitude Sports Center in Butte
WILLIAM R. SALLAZ

Cool down after the Sweet Pea Road Race in Bozeman   WILLIAM R. SALLAZ

Wildflowers beneath Mount Rockwell, Glacier National Park   MICHAEL S. SAMPLE

Summer-sleek mule deer buck with antlers covered by "velvet"   ART WOLFE

Mountain ladys-slippers, rare wild orchids   MICHAEL S. SAMPLE

*E*very time we go off into the

wilderness, we are looking for that

perfect primitive Eden. This time

we have found it.

Wallace Stegner, from "Crossing Into Eden" in
Where the Bluebird Sings to the Lemonade Springs

East Rosebud River emptying into East Rosebud Lake in the Beartooth Mountains   MICHAEL S. SAMPLE

Close encounter with a scar-faced grizzly bear   MIKE LOGAN

Camping rule in grizzly country: suspend the food bag
MICHAEL S. SAMPLE

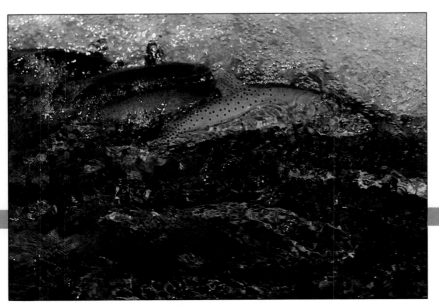

Spawning cutthroat trout   MICHAEL S. SAMPLE

S uddenly a thicket cracked just to

my right and there out of a trembling

mass of green leaves rose the head and

shoulders of the biggest bear I ever saw.

Grizzled and silvery, the fur flowed

down off her head to her huge sloping

shoulders, one arm raising up with the

claws out in the air, and seeing that, a

great rush of fear hit me like a splash

of cold water.

David Thomson, from *In the Shining Mountains*

Tree-lined Shonkin Creek carving through the prairie between Fort Benton and Square Butte   MICHAEL S. SAMPLE

*T*his eastern section of the country is a land of extremes. It gets less than twenty inches of

rainfall a year. It can get bitterly cold in the winter and desert-hot in the summer. Its winds are

ocean-like in character, just as the plains themselves are ocean-like in their sweep to the

horizon. Over this vast, treeless country the winds are little retarded by friction, and hence they

blow with remarkable uniformity and relatively high velocity. "Does the wind blow this way

here all the time?" asked the eastern visitor. "No, Mister," replied the cowboy, "it'll maybe blow

this way for a week or ten days, and then it'll take a change and blow like hell for a while."

K. Ross Toole, from *Montana: An Uncommon Land*

Sego lilies reaching towards the Big Sky east of Billings   MICHAEL S. SAMPLE

Sailing an ice boat on wind-swept Priest Butte Lake near Choteau
NEAL & MARY JANE MISHLER

The town of Livingston with peaks of the Absaroka-Beartooth Wilderness just beyond   SALVATORE J. VASPOL

*C*ivilization and culture have never quite caught up in this great region.

The rivers were bridged in strategic places, and the soil felt the plow. But

wilderness was never really far from the windowpane....

K. Ross Toole, from *Montana: An Uncommon Land*

Flower-carpeted hillside on Mount Jumbo, on the edge of Missoula   DIANE ENSIGN

Holter Lake, last of a series of three reservoirs on the Missouri River near Helena   MICHAEL S. SAMPLE

Mule deer buck and antelope sharing space near Gardiner   MICHAEL S. SAMPLE

Calypso orchids blooming in Glacier National Park   TOM & PAT LEESON

"A Potter's Shrine" and "Tile X" at the Archie Bray Foundation in Helena   DARRIN A. SCHREDER

St. Helena Cathedral, completed in 1924   JOHN REDDY

Tour boat plying the waters of Swiftcurrent Lake beneath Mount Gould in Glacier National Park   TOM & PAT LEESON

*M*ontanans have room to live, to breathe, and above all, to think—

to think with a breadth of view which goes to the far horizon and beyond.

Vast and empty space and high mountains may isolate a population,

but they open the minds of a people.

Mike Mansfield, from the introduction

Fair day on the fairways at Polson Country Club on Flathead Lake   MICHAEL JAVORKA

Dancer in Helena   WILLIAM R. SALLAZ

Cycling Pattee Canyon near Missoula   JOHN REDDY

Foothills of the Absaroka Mountains between Big Timber and Livingston   MICHAEL S. SAMPLE

Black baldy and calf   MICHAEL S. SAMPLE

Herding cattle on the Centennial Cattle Drive   MICHAEL S. SAMPLE

Camas flowers, whose bulbs were a valuable food for Native Americans and early explorers, in the Big Hole Valley   MICHAEL S. SAMPLE

Ranch country beneath the Elkhorn Mountains near Townsend   MIKE LOGAN

I don't think I ever knew the real meaning of neighborliness until I came to

Montana.... In this country,...you don't send flowers, you take an extra

hotwater bottle, a bag of ice or a change of bed linen. Sometimes the only help

you can give is releasing a worried mother from the kitchen, for ranch work

must go on, illness or no. But whatever there is to do, you do it gladly,

knowing full well that when trouble strikes, the same will be done for you.

Hughie Call, from "The Rural Telephone" in *The Last Best Place*

Sunset along the Rocky Mountain Front near Kiowa MICHAEL S. SAMPLE

Ready to ride MICHAEL S. SAMPLE

Farrier fitting a logging horse near Condon WILLIAM MUNOZ

Wrinkled foothills of the Beartooth Mountains near Absarokee   MICHAEL S. SAMPLE

*T*o *fly over Montana—east or west—is to recognize how little man has*

really changed the country. The occasional ribbon of a highway or railway,

lost as it is upon the plain or buried in the folds of the mountains, is poor

testimony to man's conquest of nature. The occasional town or city, laid out

with incongruous geometry, does little to take the edge off the impression

of impenetrable wilderness.

K. Ross Toole, from *Montana: An Uncommon Land*

Dawn's first glow on the rugged Crazy Mountains   MICHAEL S. SAMPLE

Lush growth on avalanche slopes below Heavy Runner Peak in Glacier National Park   MICHAEL S. SAMPLE

Swinging on a campground pump, Kootenai National Forest
DONALD M. JONES

Symbols of Montana's wilderness: grizzly sow and cub
TOM & PAT LEESON

Grinnell Lake colored by glacial silt from Grinnell Glacier in Glacier National Park MICHAEL JAVORKA

Expansive view from the summit of the Pryor Mountains in south-central Montana   MICHAEL S. SAMPLE

*T*his is the land *"where the sky comes down the same distance all around"* and those who live in it love it—most of the time. There is something compelling about its distances and sweep. Here there is elbowroom. The land is only monotonous to those who do not know it. It is, in fact, ever changing. When there is moisture it can get incredibly green. In the autumn it gets tawny, and swift-moving cloud shadows give it motion. The wind carries the pungently clean odor of sage. Nowhere except at sea is there quite the same subtlety of color, quite the same feeling of vastness.

K. Ross Toole, from *Montana: An Uncommon Land*

Rolling prairie hills at the Little Bighorn Battlefield National Monument   MICHAEL S. SAMPLE

One of Montana's far horizons beyond a jack-leg fence in the Big Hole Valley   MICHAEL S. SAMPLE

O ften we need to be reminded of our blessings. With a fresh eye and

renewed appreciation we need to see the great roll of our plains, the majesty

of our mountains, the beauty of our valleys. All of it—every fruitful field,

every stretch of grazing land, every spire, every forest, every far horizon—

is a wonder. What places offer more? What places as much?

A. B. Guthrie, Jr., from *"Land: Use and Abuse"*

Autumn-colored western larch spiking a conifer forest above McDonald Creek, Glacier National Park   MICHAEL JAVORKA

Clearing autumn storm on Going-to-the-Sun Mountain, Glacier National Park   MICHAEL S. SAMPLE

Fall foliage in the foothills of the Absaroka Mountains   MICHAEL S. SAMPLE

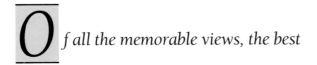f all the memorable views, the best

have been framed by Montana windows.

William Hjortsberg from "The View from My Window"
in *Montana Spaces*

Northern lights dancing above Flathead Lake   MICHAEL S. SAMPLE

Alpenglow glow on McDonald Peak in the Mission Mountains   WILLIAM MUNOZ

Winter dawn coming over the Big Belt Mountains near Townsend   DARRIN A. SCHREDER

Autumn in the Two Medicine Valley, Glacier National Park   MICHAEL JAVORKA

M ontana is...something else, something that makes others love the state

though they recognize its shortcomings, that gives to visitors the sense of

living in a different, less fretful, and a better world. It is here one feels an

individual superiority to event, a be-damned attitude toward mischance, a

freedom from or ascendancy over the anxieties that press so hard elsewhere.

Montanans somehow stay on top of life.

A. B. Guthrie, Jr., from "Montana" in *Holiday* magazine

A portion of the Garden Wall, Glacier National Park   MICHAEL JAVORKA

Birch trees   MICHAEL S. SAMPLE

Fall fishing on the Yellowstone River   MICHAEL S. SAMPLE

Water-carved patterns in Big Salmon Creek, Flathead National Forest   MICHAEL S. SAMPLE

Grizzly bear on a backcountry hillside   MICHAEL S. SAMPLE

Ripe huckleberries   MICHAEL JAVORKA

Wind-whipped clouds shrouding the moon over the Bridger Mountains
DARRIN A. SCHREDER

Gray wolves in northern Montana   WILLIAM MUNOZ

*L*and. *Wildness. Life itself. They are inseparable in Montana. There is no other possibility here. Life, in the control of raw and awesome nature as it is in few other places in America, demands it. It is for this you come; for this you stay; or because of it, you leave. It is on the edge of wildness that the American spirit is most at home. For some of us, it takes a long time to realize there is a home. Yet, whenever it happens, when we arrive, we recognize it at once.*

Ruth Rudner, from *Greetings From Wisdom, Montana*

Photographer's shadow in Makoshika State Park
MICHAEL S. SAMPLE

THEY MADE IT POSSIBLE

Montana–the name itself evokes visions of snow-capped peaks, golden wheatfields, and cowboys riding the open range. Yet, Montana is more than that. It's a spirit that people have been trying to capture for years through literature and art. The photographs in this book, highlighted by quotes from the best writings about Montana, celebrate this spirit and the enduring beauty of the last best state.

Montana: The Last Best Place would not have been possible without the skills and efforts of the photographers listed here. Their hard work and diligent pursuit of excellence sets their work apart from all the rest.

To all of the photographers who contributed to *Montana: The Last Best Place*, thank you.

Michael S. Sample, Bill Schneider
Publishers, Falcon Press

PHOTOGRAPHERS IN MONTANA: THE LAST BEST PLACE

Bob Allen
Erwin & Peggy Bauer
Denver A. Bryan
Linda Cauble
Michael S. Crummett
Bill Cunningham
Paul Dix
Diane Ensign
Jeff Henry
Michael Javorka
Donald M. Jones
Bud Journey
Tom & Pat Leeson
Mike Logan
Neal & Mary Jane Mishler
William Munoz
John Reddy
William R. Sallaz
Michael S. Sample
Darrin A. Schreder
George Schuyler
Scott Spiker
Larry Ulrich
Jeff Vanuga
Salvatore J. Vaspol
Art Wolfe
Garry Wunderwald

Published as a tribute to the Montana Historical Society Press book, *The Last Best Place: A Montana Anthology*, in accord with the Montana Historical Society.

Copyright © 1992 by Falcon Press Publishing Co., Inc., Helena and Billings, Montana

Editing, design, typesetting, and other prepress work by Falcon Press, Helena, Montana. Binding and printing in Korea.

Library of Congress Number: 92-72803

ISBN 1-56044-151-8

For extra copies of this book please check with your local bookstore, or write to Falcon Press, P.O. Box 1718, Helena, MT 59624. You may also call toll-free 1-800-582-2665.

ACKNOWLEDGMENTS

The publisher gratefully acknowledges the following sources:

Pages 21, 27, 55, and 61 from "More Than Skin Deep" by Glenn Law in *Montana Spaces*. Copyright 1988 by the Montana Land Reliance; Nick Lyons Books, New York.

Page 25 from "A River Runs Through It" by Norman Maclean in *The Last Best Place*. Copyright 1988; The Montana Historical Society, Helena, Montana. Reprinted from *A River Runs Through It*, University of Chicago Press.

Page 28 from *Great Plains* by Ian Frazier. Copyright 1989; Farrar/Straus/Giroux, New York.

Page 30 from "In Spite of Distance" by Ralph Beer in *Montana Spaces*. Copyright 1988 by the Montana Land Reliance; Nick Lyons Books, New York.

Pages 34, 72, and 76 from "The Big Sky" by A. B. Guthrie, Jr., in *The Last Best Place*. Copyright 1988; The Montana Historical Society, Helena, Montana.

Page 38 from "Eclipse" by David Long in *The Last Best Place*. Copyright 1988; The Montana Historical Society, Helena, Montana. Reprinted from *Home Fires*, University of Illinois Press, 1982.

Page 42 from "Homestead Days in Montana" by Pearl Price Robertson in *The Last Best Place*. Copyright 1988; The Montana Historical Society, Helena, Montana.

Page 44 Luther Standing Bear, Oglala Sioux in *Montana Outdoors*. November/December 1981.

Pages 48 and 68 from "A Matter of Blood" by Scott Hibbard in *Montana Spaces*. Copyright 1988 by the Montana Land Reliance; Nick Lyons Books, New York.

Page 64 from "A Toad in Hell" by Dan Cushman in *The Last Best Place*. Copyright 1988; The Montana Historical Society, Helena, Montana.

Page 80 from *Montana, Tourist Edition* by Department of Agriculture, Labor and Industry, 1921; State of Montana, Helena, Montana.

Page 87 from "Crossing Into Eden" by Wallace Stegner in *Where the Bluebird Sings to the Lemonade Springs*. Copyright 1992; Random House, New York.

Page 89 from *In the Shining Mountains* by David Thomson. Copyright 1979; Knopf, New York.

Pages 90, 92, 102, 106, and 120 from *Montana: An Uncommon Land* by K. Ross Toole. Copyright 1959; University of Oklahoma Press, Norman, Oklahoma.

Page 100 from "The Rural Telephone" by Hughie Call in *The Last Best Place*. Copyright 1988; The Montana Historical Society, Helena, Montana.

Page 108 from "Land: Use and Abuse" by A. B. Guthrie, Jr. October 15, 1974.

Page 111 from "The View from My Window" by William Hjortsberg in *Montana Spaces*. Copyright 1988 by the Montana Land Reliance; Nick Lyons Books, New York.

Page 114 from "Montana" by A. B. Guthrie, Jr., in *Holiday* magazine. September, 1950.

Page 117 from *Greetings From Wisdom, Montana* by Ruth Rudner. Copyright 1989; Fulcrum, Inc., Golden, Colorado.

ABOUT MIKE MANSFIELD

The introduction to *Montana: The Last Best Place* was written by Mike Mansfield, a distinguished Montanan who has forged a remarkable career in public service. Mansfield represented Montana in the U.S. House of Representatives and Senate for thirty-four years, including sixteen years as Senate Majority Leader. After retiring from the Senate in 1977, he served as U.S. Ambassador to Japan for twelve years. Senator Mansfield spent most of his childhood in Great Falls, and before he entered politics he was a professor of history and political science at the University of Montana. The Senator currently resides in Washington, D.C., where he is an advisor on Far Eastern affairs.

Watching a sunset on the Missouri River near Craig   JOHN REDDY

Whatever else has changed, the sky has not—its pale

immensity in winter, its blue depth in summer, the great

white fists of its clouds, and the fierce ecstasy of its sunsets.

Montana is still high, wide, handsome, and remote. There

are many ways of looking at it and many ways of feeling

about it. And there is room for all the ways.

K. Ross Toole, from *Montana: An Uncommon Land*